OUTSIDE THE LINES

A collection of poetry

written by

LISA SOMERSET

OUTSIDE THE LINES

Copyright © 2024 Lisa Somerset
All rights reserved.

All rights reserved. No part of this publication may be reproduced, stored in a retrieval system, distributed or transmitted in any form or by any means – electronic, mechanical, photocopying, and recording or otherwise – without prior written permission from the author, except in the case of brief quotations in book reviews and other noncommercial uses permitted by copyright law. If you would like to use material from the book (other than for review purposes), prior written permission must be obtained by contacting the author at lnk.bio/lisa_somerset_poems.

Thank you for your support of the author's rights.

ISBN: 979-83-32730-48-1 (paperback)
ISBN: 979-83-32731-01-3 (hardcover)

Cover Design and Illustration by: Rein G.
Layout Design by: Rein G.
www.fiverr.com/reindrawthings

Dedicated to my very supportive family:
husband Doug (my rock),

daughter Alana (my anchor),
mom Lore (my guiding light)

and dad Ralph (my creative influence,
now living in the stars).

CONTENTS

Introduction	1
Got Milk?	3
a comfort in knowing	4
what I like	5
anole	7
Photography	9
Wandering Spirits	10
Tracing Back	11
Off-kilter	13
Doggedly Devoted	17
Doesn't Add Up	18
tales of centuries	19
Three Course Meal	21
my babe	23
complete	25
Did I Say	27
astronomy	29
Hot/Cold	33
Light heaviness	34
inside out	35

Keep it small	37
No Picasso	39
In we come... out we go...	40
childhood transition	41
Perspective	43
slow down	47
Go Through the Grind	48
Hard to describe	49
Glamour Monsters	51
miss ing	53
geometric	54
Flavor	55
Consumers	57
aqua relief	61
facing silence	62
Yesterday's Youth	63
heavy lids	65
Otherly	67
Mind Gobble	68
be satisfied	69
cancel cancel culture	71

The Absence of "Hello"	75
numb	76
Homo Sapien Syndrome	77
Outsiders	79
All There Is	81
not that simple	82
a dream	84
butterfly	85
Depression	89
Not A-OK	90
...just passing	91
Literature	93
Rewild Me	95
together	96
somewhere in between	97
museic	98
first impressions	103
shells and shadows	104
Never-ending...	105
It's Our Fault	107
Atoms of Dad	109
Wouldn't It Be Great If...	110

Balance	112
Cell phones	113
Sleep	117
passion fruit	118
Thesaurus Poet	120
drying flowers	123
far away	125
Voltage	126
Sad But True	127
Uh Oh	129
Stay the course	133
Make It Quick	134
Aging	135
Our Entirety	137
Find Your Flow	139
What It Means to Rain	140
little tiny us	141
Youness	143
Acknowledgements	146
About the Author	147

INTRODUCTION

I've written poems as a hobby on and off throughout my teen and adult life. To me, there is something so satisfying about those random lightbulb moments, when your mind tells you: "Okay, it's time to write!" Then subsequently to produce a piece which can mean one thing to me, but possibly something quite different to others reading it, is both exciting and rewarding. Poetry is very diverse and so much can be taken from it. A gift that keeps on giving! I always call poetry the "art of words."

Outside The Lines is my chosen book title because I very much respect individuals who don't adhere to stereotypes, fit in boxes or bend to "societal norms." Props to those who overcome adversity and rejoice in being their own person, choosing to live life outside the lines.

Hopefully you, the reader, enjoy reading my poems as much as I've enjoyed writing them. I don't have set themes and just go with the flow regarding subject matter, so there is enough variety to suit many a literature lover's palate.

LISA SOMERSET

Got Milk?

Such calmness as your
Hand   s m o o t h e s   over mine
And before the moment is
Captured you withdraw as if in spite
You leave me standing
Replace that delicate touch with
Icicles of isolation and I shudder
In my mind
Calcification of thoughts
You've hardened me as I am no
Longer the same lover of
Love
And sitting at the table
The box of cookies brings
Me back to reality
So I grab another Oreo
Left thirsting for
        Something and a glass of milk

a comfort in knowing

you've been by my side since the   beginning
one step ahead   to learn from   love with
so reassuring   the internal cord of connection
                       symbiosis of selves
       ~a feeling of wholeness~
providing guidance
      inspiration   minus interference
         allowing me interpretive imitation and room
    to grow
                     all for which I thank you

what I like

I like
what we are
I like
what we aren't
I like the similarity of
our differences
your black in my
white
our grey
enjoy the
running of lips and fingertips
together and
apart
I like to touch
as you touch me
I touch you
when we become one
no more or less than
the other
then that is what
I like

LISA SOMERSET

anole

a catapulting mind
rearranging
recreating
what others yet have not
perfected
mind seeks not perfection but
immortality of
knowledge and eternal
freedom
as the soul overthrows the
body
and lives
a hermit in explicit
ponderings
residing in the carnal cleavage of
the brain
so I would enjoy having the
power to lose my
head
as the anole does its
tail
to run away
happily without it
living on instinct and indifference
alone

LISA SOMERSET

Photography

We stop time
When the
Shutter captures its image
Keep a little piece of yesterday for
Tomorrow
A segment of the past for
The future
We are immortal in our
Pictures
Sustained by mere
Clicks of a button
A here and now thing
Only forever
Camera
Flash
Keeping the night day in
Our memories
Allowing us to retain what
We would otherwise forget
The developing of film and the
Developing of ourselves
A unique intermingling of
Plastic and flesh caught in
The moment
What a brilliant
Invention

Wandering Spirits

Raining hands over
Scattered bodies
We're all searching   seeking
An ultimate happiness
A profound ecstasy
Robbing the night of
Dreams and wishes
Once parted with
Taking back what should
Be ours
And awaking to nothing but
Ourselves
Seduced by optimism
Raped by negativity
All feel defeated in
The end when faced with
Reality

Tracing Back

Memories lie
Retain all imperfections
Reveal only the good
Leave one wondering
Was something left out
Forgotten
Displaced
Or merely erased to hide the pain
?

LISA SOMERSET

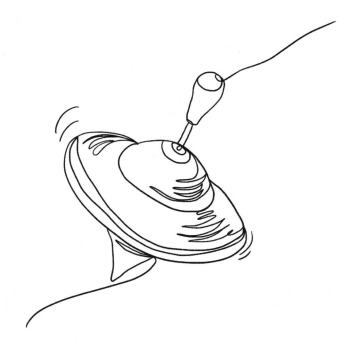

Off-kilter

Like a spinning top which
loses its centre
we are veering toward
unknown territory
unchartered waters
Our dirty touch on this world
tainting the delicate balance
of nature and nurture
While the hands of science
reach pleadingly for us to help and
restore
We run predictably in the other direction to
bury our heads in safe sands
away from awareness and accountability
Leaving the wild to fester in our
grim careless leftovers
drowning under our crass irresponsibility

"Poetry has but one rule: write."

LISA SOMERSET

Doggedly Devoted

You are anatomically designed to
drill to our very cores
via signals expressions sounds
You unleash in us all kinds of
emotions and are so very
engaging
Astonishing and endearing with
that fulfilling fluffiness and
charismatic charm
We're hooked and you know
this and love us right
back
There is nothing more pure than
that which you
give with the reach of a
paw or lick of the
hand

Doesn't Add Up

They travel the world
trashing beautiful destinations
swarming lush green lands
Just to make their
memories
Have their
holidays
While taking natural beauty in their hands and
killing it
With souvenirs they take souls
The lifeblood
each flower
coral
creature
from its home
Slowly destroying earth's ecosystem
Until all they'll have left to photograph
are polluted skies
fossils and ash

tales of centuries

       fall before me as they
reveal   explicitly dissect what
those preceding us dealt with
      and I welcome this
newfound past as our ancestors turn
jaded pages so we may
      in time   find the differences and
uniquenesses that bring ourselves and history
      together so intricately--
          antiquity's wounds though nearly mended
obtain a piece of my heart   as I feel for those taken by
        war   famine   disease
    before our history became ours
and these tales of centuries
      make for noteworthy occasions
    as we and as those before us
      celebrate in the refining qualities of
history pieced and pasted in the present
      of our minds

LISA SOMERSET

Three Course Meal

You must have been devastatingly hungry
as you ate your words with much humble pie
for dinner
but not before swallowing large mouthfuls of pride
for a starter
and finishing with eating a touch of dirt
for dessert
before you settled the bill

LISA SOMERSET

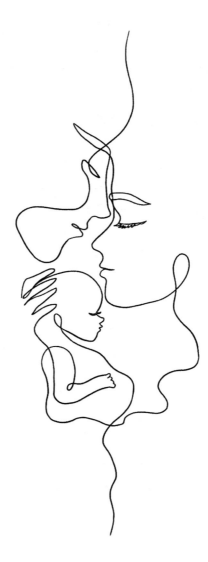

my babe

a breakthrough
1+1=you (!)
my little something
special
formed from
love and
stardust
it's amazing baby
how you are

        a smidgen of us both
yet
        a being all your own

unique
poetry   words cannot describe
how I adore you and your
becoming
a wonderful wonder

a breakthrough like no other
our soul masterpiece

LISA SOMERSET

and like art
you take in our hearts
through our eyes
envelope us

we are your admirers
forever

complete

the words he speaks convince me
that what I feel is right
it seems like I have loved him
from the very first night
he comes from distant land
far out of my reach
yet if by consolation
a lesson this does teach
it teaches of desire
of love and feeling new
inside me burns a fire
this I know is true
he brings about such changes
I will never be the same
he eases all my hunger
takes away the pain
now never am I empty
he made my half quite whole
it's almost as if unconsciously
this was my aspired goal
to find a love so treasured
that distance not denies
these heartfelt emotions
always on the rise
we find in us the truth

which behind the shadows sings
of joy and prosperity
which only love can bring

Did I Say

Did I say
I could write poetry because
I can't
Concentration
Flow
Description
I am not so intellectual
So imaginative
So free-spirited
Do you see me
Tumbling words onto the paper in my mind
Like some shooting stars from the sky
Shuffling the cards
Of my soul
Purging rhythm
Formed of love, serenity and ideals
Am I seething in your mind
When I laugh and write about
Loose ends and beaten hearts
And is a smirk left
Upon your
I'm such a smart, funny, handsome man face
When you see

LISA SOMERSET

My
So I can't write poetry worth diddly poems
Did I say I could move you with my
Writing
Because I can't
And did I say it doesn't bother me that
Poems don't
Plunge into my thoughts
And create
Such feeling that I could drown in your eyes
Melt in your smile
Lose control in your passionate touch
No
Did I say I could write poetry because
I can't.

astronomy

a radiation
solicitation of the stars
coming for me from your
eyes
meteor showers as your fingers
probe and unwrap me
remove the rings of Saturn
I am naked
while all of Orion examines me
my mind feels
weightless
as you are the first to take
a step on the surface
of my being
and I feel the glory of an
astronaut
as you submerge me in your
galaxy

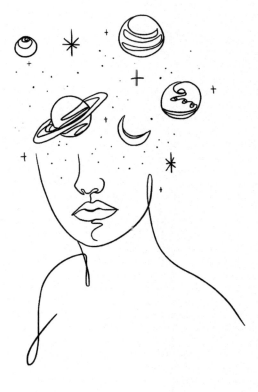

"Your youness is your trueness."

LISA SOMERSET

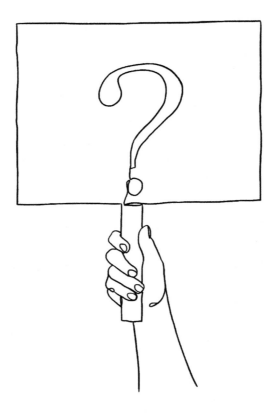

Hot/Cold

Make up/your mind/or do you just blend/You were someone then/and another now/Who are you/Stand true and tall/Never forsake your values/You are better than that/I hope

Light heaviness

Wanting more
Platinum as opposed to silver
Actions in place of words
Not a good feeling
Rather upsetting in fact
Stolen peeks at grass on the greener side
Yet any feeling is better than none
Surely sometimes
Never always
Aware of a weight upon my shoulders
I do not wish to bear
Tired of that pull
The strain
At the "be" of "becoming" yet no further
Progressive digression
Blind spot glimpses of possibilities
Light-hearted visions of gold-plated dreams
Not easy to deal with
Those growth holes leaving gaps inside
Either for leverage or lowering
Completion or contemplation
Depending
So much heavier than light

inside out

inside I'm all thoughts and dreams
outside you are what I seem
to be
saying everything I feel
and you are so very real
don't know why I tried to
deny it
thought about it
but it's true
the outside of me is you
had no courage
had no fire
but you freed my desires
got me living
let me shine through
now I'm outside being me with
you

LISA SOMERSET

Keep it small

Your circle
Don't let many in
Be wise
With numbers   come complexities
Deny drama entering your
Safe place
Keep it simple
And real
Beware of gift givers   many bring hidden
Agendas
See behind the smiles
Read between the lines
Cherish compositions made of
Honesty
Truth
Genuine love

LISA SOMERSET

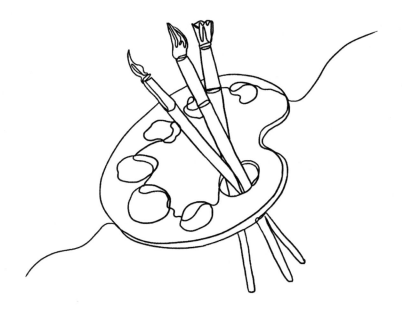

No Picasso

Gentle ribbons of color
Ripple all around me
Paint
Wrap me in rainbows
Yet somehow I remain pale
Indifferent to the differences outside me
No change inside
Still black and white
I long to have some inner brightness
A pastel dabbed soul to contain me
But it seems I am an artist
Whose palette was never filled

In we come...   out we go...

But wait (!)
How lucky are we
to take part in what
plenty will never bear witness
This short but sweet spell
of experiencing
observing
existing
How many are so fortunate
to see the light of dying stars (?)
To feel their feet graze the surface of
an organic spinning orb (?)
What a lark
Such a privilege
We are here
We are alive

childhood transition

these children we call ourselves
they play hopscotch
love gumballs and rootbeer floats
marshmallows too.

these children we call ourselves
lose touch of reality and instead stick to
a yellowhappy world of fun
gripping each other's hands
and laughing.

these children we call ourselves
dread naptime and can't get enough of
the play escape during recess
climbing the monkey bars
and playing hide-and-go-seek.

these children we call ourselves
release their spirits into
a wonderland of
shimmering china waiting to be
broken and reshaped
place full of teddy bears and
toy cars.

these children we call ourselves
are just adults wishing on
four-leaf clovers and
dancing to the sounds of
memories.

Perspective

Poetry had words with Fiction
She told him she felt overlooked and
Undervalued
Always in Fiction's shadow
Gaining less of an audience
While giving all of herself
Feeling her growth was stunted
By Fiction's fortune
To which Fiction nodded thoughtfully
He then responded
That Poetry embodies each of the arts
She is in songs, stories, paintings
How could she possibly feel so small
When she is a most enviable writing style
~She is all around us~
This to which Poetry was silent
Pleasantly lost for words

"Always add a dash of sassy
and a dose of classy..."

LISA SOMERSET

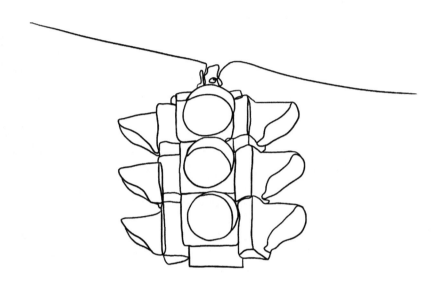

slow down

we're on this superhighway
of life
it's all so fast
and stop signs
for those we
barely pause
I almost miss being
in the passenger seat
taking in the view from
another angle
the peaceful side
a safe side
this green light of living
frightens me
don't want to gogogo
want to stay
stay
stay
we should have more time to pass
through the yellow or
just sit at the red
and think
let life catch its breath
so we'll be ready to safely cross
the upcoming intersection
into the
future

Go Through the Grind

It is invigorating to feel down
        As from sullen lows come gratifying highs
Each day that we are sinking
              Gives rise for us to swim
Grab the controls when you feel a lull
                  Confront the maddening turmoil
Watch and see your amazing abilities unfold
                Your mind skilfully shifting gears

Hard to describe

It's not writing when you're
feeling it
Emotion more than
words Like
emptying my soul on
paper But more sacred than it
sounds Something
that connects the outs of me with
the in Helps
me understand more or
less the alls and ends of everything No
something or other Maybe
nothing but none the less a
retreat A
let go and be An
attempt if nothing
more

LISA SOMERSET

Glamour Monsters

We are glamour monsters
Give me materials colours styles
I want black purple brown green and white with a dab of
ooh la la
Flaunt those boots flats flip flops heels lace ups sandals
slip-on shoes
Wear that v-neck turtleneck scoop neck décolleté cleavage-
showing sleeveless top
Strut my jeans flares bootcut capri ¾ length
shorts skorts skirts
So ~~G L A M O R O U S~~
symmetric asymmetric any way all ways
sexy slutty skimpy scruffy safe worn torn
nets tights garters suspenders stockings knee highs
belts boas hats caps berets
lace satin leather shiny sheer showy
broaches bracelets chokers rings necklaces jewels beads
bling blam (!)
do it use it sew it snip it make it lovvvely
long hair short hair bob or fringe shave or perm
pop that compact slap on that lip smack
line those lashy lids cherry those cheeks
plush flush fiery fierce glittery glossy

LISA SOMERSET

    kick my heels up   wear my designer frock
          sip my Starbucks
      god how I   love my luck
          tickle me pink
      make up   make me up
         mannequin me baby.

miss   ing

she   young woman
liked of being loved/loving
         lacked of being learned
man   his love energy splattered over her vessel-led heart
she submerged finds streaks untenured/untouched
         leaps beyond the beating organ
     outsidethelines within her
         (to find what/if she was missing(?)
         wanting more/or less?)
looking for the answers

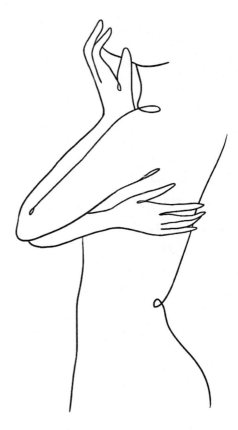

geometric

it's an odd fulfilment
between you and me
a circular
contentment
rotating and revolving
helping us grow
further near to
our apartness
away from ourselves
and closer to
each other
a tension-driving
experience
challenging and
double-edged
it's that force
that keeps the
circle turning
keeping us
together

Flavor

I've tasted their life energy
And find it not
Bitter but by no means
Sweet
A variety suiting some
Other's appetite not
My own
Funny how
Un/appealing things/people can be how
You don't know until you
Try
But after sampling the grapes of
Wrath I go back to
Oranges

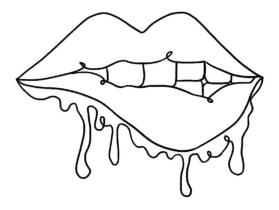

Consumers

I see the greed dripping from their
grease-laden lips
See the selfishness clenched in those
fat-fingered fists
Credit cards poised   ready to strike
Air thick with their wanting   their craving
These gorgers   these takers
Devouring our world
bit by bit
bite by bite
binge by binge
Unhappy unless consuming in
some way   shape   or form
Desiring so much more than needed
Human locusts   driven by excess
Walking in droves among us
Indifferent in their self-serving bubbles
Diminishing finite resources
Eating the rest of us alive

"You're a sensational survivor."

aqua relief

welcoming rain
splashing its water over my eyes
down my neck, upon my chest
letting the coolness of it captivate me
refresh my mind
and wash thoughts of you away
droplets ripple over me
consume me
once we frolicked in this water
you embraced me in this water
honeyed liquid we called "love"
now this water plummets down my body
ground seeps in the remainder
as it cascades back up to, into
the watershed of my soul
our waters separate
the rivers streams branch off in opposite directions
and flow deep into trenches light years away
maybe someday
our waters will resurface
and create an ocean of elation.

facing silence

he wrapped his fingers in her fingers
she wrapped her fingers in his fingers
both better when entwined
no need for common chatter
wasted words serving useless
silence so much better
leaving more to the imagination

Yesterday's Youth

You got my years
Honey
Not my yearning
You got my body
Darling
Not my soul
My mistake
Not my glory
Empty time
Sweetie
Tickless tocking
Did you like our
Hollow union (?)
Grow from our
Distance (?)
Further yourself from our
Apartness (?)
Or just turn numb in
Indifference (?)
A terrible mismatch
Baby
Sad to say

Opposite characters
An unlucky meeting
Much of a muchness
And for nothing
Dear
But to say we did

heavy lids

open and release me
ecstatic
dramatic
visions flow as I follow
something so moving
double-take
these wonders
this world before me
such feeling inside me
look left
look forward
look right
heavy lids
shut and withdraw me
darkness seeps as I sink
something so
slowly
taunting
flashback images
this world behind me
such feeling outside me
blind left
blind forward
blind right

eyes
heavy lids
wide open
as he says he loves me

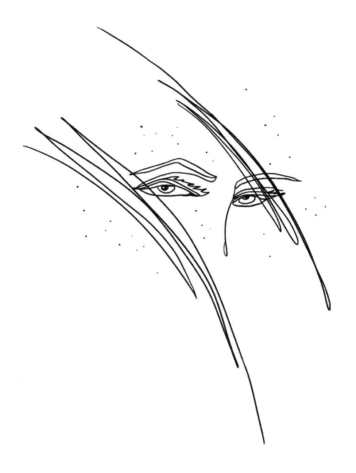

Otherly

She does life superficially
    with her fake eyelashes
    hair extensions
    enhanced breasts
    inflated fish lips
Desperate to receive much
    positive attention
    envy
    praise
But we all see her otherness
those eyeballs rolled inside her head
solely focused on herself
Her fake tan epidermis flipped inside out
exposing veiny bloody weaknesses
She isn't comfortable in her own skin
This whole feigned formation
one fractured messy mass
A woman who is everything
but herself

Mind Gobble

Feed me more of what
you've got
Spinning your lines around my fork
like pasta
Throw some thoughts in which
cut deep
I'll knaw that new-found knowledge to
the bone
Drinking and drawing in
your refreshing perspectives
Ingesting fresh views and
organic ideas
Filling up on your
entire being
With you I'll always
have room for
seconds

be satisfied

these words you speak are toxic
as they roll teasingly off your
tongue and
taunt me

what I relish is placid
ludicrously lonely
but I like it
so why try and
change me--
conform my
consistence?
because you in turn
push me farther and farther away

see
I am gone
and you are left
trying to convert your feeble
coercion

LISA SOMERSET

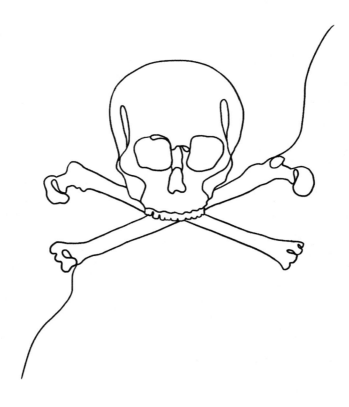

cancel cancel culture

before it's too late
      (or are we too far gone?)
the silencing   erosion
erasing   all for what
but to suit agendas   by means of
manipulation   and control
poisoning our society
taking away what is real
replacing actuality with fiction   fabrication
altering our reality
words   histories   edited   deleted
just to appease the criers   the destroyers
day by day our freedoms diminish
our speech   our rights
    ~don't say that
        don't do this~
a handful of humans damaging our
foreseeable future
(how did we get so weak?)
so we must stand tall   and for what's right
disallow this corrupt toxicity to encase us
hold tight to our freedoms   truths
before they are   no longer ours

"Her heart is both predator and prey."

LISA SOMERSET

The Absence of "Hello"

It was the other day that I
Walked through the door
Feeling unsure and seemingly
Untied
Stepped into our apartment
Where started just two dreamers
Searching for some perfect world
We knew we'd never find
Looked around our little hideout
To realize the presence of
A suitcase
Not yours
Not mine
Not wanted here
And later when I asked you
Where it came from
Your reply was confused
But your fixed glare on the square looter
Was insistent
As somewhere near/far from us I heard a
"Goodbye."

numb

so far from all I'm   nothing
inside a vast hollowness
deteriorating
thoughts fired
but they're blanks
placebos of destruction
I feel lost
my brain a displaced placement
numbness fusing good with bad
sad with happy
right with wrong
it's unnerving
calm in the midst of chaos
surrendering to solitude
from falling to fallen
when will I start feeling again (?)

Homo Sapien Syndrome

I'm not depressed
Not negative
Realistic
is different
very
Don't suffer fools gladly
Refuse to repress thoughts
comments
This is life
live it
think it
say it
Not rebellion but I'm no
societal zombie
Vehemently detest
followers
Sheep amongst their herd
I'm not cynical
just observant
Not a hater
just people-picky
They push me to my limits
sugar-coated posers
Living behind masks of doubtless gullibility

LISA SOMERSET

Will they SEE their world eventually
smell the pollution
not just the flowers
Why are they so afraid to break their smiles (?)

Outsiders

I like your
forward thinking in this
behind world

Both of us dropping under
the radar in so that
we may fully see

I'll take the wrist slaps
You'll take the knuckle raps

This pair favouring unpopular
reality over in demand blind faith

Free thinkers on a planet with
invisible bars

LISA SOMERSET

All There Is

Your whispers do that to me
they sing straight through my skin

Your presence is my pastime
I'm taking it all in

Before us yesterdays meant nothing
now my tomorrows belong to you

This heart it keeps on beating
knowing only what is true

Down to my bones you get my essence
we're steeped in each other's cores

I feel you with me even in your absence
resounding through my every pore

not that simple

easy to say I don't
care
hard to admit how much I
do
emotions
crazy
crazy
emotions
you watch me drown
in this frazzled
ocean of feelings
my latent
lifeguard
help me
save me
love me
I need your heart to
live
need your eyes to
see
need your lips to
breathe
yet it is not that

simple
as you leave me wading in
this whirlpool of life
choking in its deep
waters

a dream

silence
what I like
seem to be
you can't hear me
but you
know me
can't touch me
but you
feel me
I am the adrenaline rush with your
loud
loud
music
am the wind through your
soft
soft
hair
am your
worst nightmare

butterfly

deep inside   a heart flutters
    and there lies an unshakable feeling
  something so innocent   yet impure
      raging intoxicating
   a constriction on the verge of release
    so I let the butterfly invade me
      to color my entire soul
    it will only be too soon before
you digress   become a caterpillar
encase yourself in another's   cocoon

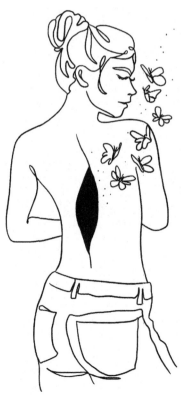

"She opened the door to yesness and never looked back."

LISA SOMERSET

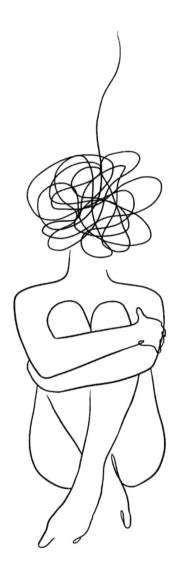

Depression

I'd do something if I weren't so
Cranky so sad so tired so blank
So faded so lost so weary could go out if
I weren't so scared so resistant so anxious so inhibited
So helpless so dispirited would
Try if I weren't so edgy so insecure so
Negative so obsessive I'd be alright if
I weren't so confused so miserable so
Depressed

Not A-OK

Don't come to me
bright-eyed and bushy-tailed
expectant of spoon-fed lies
To be wrapped up from reality
in concealing cotton wool
I will not be enabling your far-fetched visions
wearing rose-coloured glasses
And toasting to optimism's mirages
which leave most high and dry

Sugar-coating is a fool's game
suiting players who are fakers and takers

But ask me to dish out honesty
the good, the bad and the ugly
I will do so willingly
Share my glass which is as of now brim-full
at least until we drink it
And let's be nothing more or less than
nakedly and unapologetically
ourselves

…just passing

My mind takes a crash landing
A collision course through your head
And I find myself bruised
By the thoughts you keep hidden inside the
Glove compartment of your brain
For each word you haven't said
My body crashes
Bruises more and more
Cannot sustain the harsh impact
Of this accident you caused
And in the midst of all the pain
I am able to get up and
Walk away.

Literature

But not on a screen
not for me
I like to gently turn the
pressed fibrous pages   one by one
skipping over nothing   not missing a beat
patiently taking in the figments
and fragments
concocted by an
imaginative creator of
gripping textual escapes
making of the content what I will
in my own sweet time   alone but not
the book holding both
my interest and intrigue
a collaboration of   reader and writer
resulting in an omelette of
ideas mixed with
hints of eccentricity and expectation
making the perfect
meal for the mind

LISA SOMERSET

Rewild Me

Awaken this mind
      from its lengthy hibernation
      left festering in thought for all too long
Take these passive hands
      smooth from a life lived with careful
      softness
Guide them faithfully in your own
      which are richly roughened
      and reassuringly ripe
Onto greener
      wholesome pastures
Where together we'll nurture newness
      cultivating ideals planted on fertile
      foundations of optimism and instinct
Ready to begin afresh
      digging our heels and hearts into both
      land and life

together

more distant now
more fearful
such contrast between us
northern   southern poles
attraction and opposition
not equally separate nor centrally together
mostly
.
 .
  .
   .

apart

somewhere in between

the youth of spirit
and the soul of maturity
I linger
staggering between the fine lines of
darkness and piercing scorch of
light
the choice is mine
to be a somebody
or just a body
possibilities are endless
the mystery of the future and
routine consistency of the present
toss a coin
head off into the boundless realms of
tangible dreams
sink tail-end into a bottomless pit of
self pity
define fate by action
don't wait for consequence
or
stay somewhere in between

museic

my mind hangs on each note
peace in those pulses and pauses
the rises/falls make me
dizzy happy crazy content
I feel so calm
the beat
the blissful blaring
conducting me away
far
letting the rhythm relax/soothe
me
myself
suddenly that's who
I am
in the music
drums ripping my brain into chunks
guitar soothing the gaps in
between
synthesizing the soul
feel better
in a world of sounds
melody mellows me

voices

symphonic laughter

inspiring

I feel I could fly

the wings of song upon my lips

lifting me higher and

higher

and when I hit the ground

it feels a little softer

"Nature soothes her animal heart."

LISA SOMERSET

first impressions

she
upon meeting seems
small
infinitely obscure in the
world of emotion
expression
silence her defense
her tool of distinction
they find her cold
distilled
bland and indifferent
while she
soundless observer
examines
explores the
extent of their words
meaning of their motions
jumping on each detail yet
staying undisclosed
deciding
knowing just enough to
remain
remove herself
does she like what she sees (?)

shells and shadows

the lifeless body
stone cold
stillness
like a paper mache cast
solid emptiness
pallid porcelain complexion
lacking soulful energy
a heart devoid of beats
silence
silence
an anticipation of breath
followed by
eternal intermission
left only with a shell and
shadow of the
past

Never-ending…

You were like a never-ending
Friday
I remember the good times
Because you made them for me and
Somehow negatives never fit into our
Equation
It was love
Oh how we loved it
But then
Even we weren't immune to the world
Which though against our wills was
Against us
It suddenly felt more like a Monday morning
Between you and me
But coffee couldn't help
Nor a cold shower
So instead of allowing fate our
Fortunes
We took Fridays into our
Hearts and said
"Remember"

LISA SOMERSET

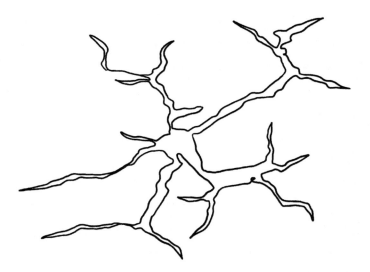

It's Our Fault

All remained beautiful
Until us
Rich and plentiful
Until us
Flourishing   unendangered
Until us
Balanced and resourceful
Until us
Natural   unintrusive
Until us
Fruitful and fair
Until us
The world was safe
Until humans

Atoms of Dad

Your final breath was not
your last   musical chairs
as exhaled atoms bound
and flow through the
air   so freely
like rhythmic gymnasts
      fleeting
           pivoting
your attachment with life
succeeds your own
mortality
as those expelled
atoms   share themselves
pass onto   into
others
recycled and reused
united by one common
link
that we are all   at some point
alive

Wouldn't It Be Great If...

Wouldn't it be great if...
upon living,
one was finally able to explain life's mysteries?
To have the power to make unique choices and not be
thought abnormal, plagued with judgement and defeat?
Wouldn't it be great if...
upon musing,
a deep thought brought to you riches and handsome lovers?
If detriment and corruption were not even words
in the nation's vocabulary,
and harmony made up the dictionary,
along with happiness and love?
Wouldn't it be great if...
wonderful dreams were our reality,
surrounded by bursts of colorful light plunging over our heads
and into a unified world of its own;
a world with only cosmos of man's final understandings--
not just the questions, but also the answers?
Wouldn't it be great if...
there was a watchful eye looking over all of us,
telling us not what we do wrong, but of our stately completions?
If its glare was focused on our glossy goodness
and not our mortal glum?
Wouldn't it be great if...

this poem were not but a poem writing of what would
be great if...,
but if writing of what is already great,
could become greater?

Balance

I'm a writer
Riding the waves of the words
Singing the songs of the silent
        You're a speaker
        Saying all through sound
        Voicing all you envision
                Together we are links
                Translators of our world
                      Conductors of insight
                      Collaborators of dreams

Cell phones

it's the ringing, dialling, endless droning
people's constant pretentious phoning
in a catatonic state
I feel the need to meditate
Johnny gets the latest ring tones
has to have them on his phone
a piece/a chunk of needless plastic
now they've all gone freaking spastic
talking in person is out of date
now it's text messaging people rate
what has this world become
all the people numb and dumb
Sue calls Mary
broken nail
Dave calls Harry
too much ale
on the move but in a circle
phones in ears turning purple
speaking nonsense/nothing but
it seems the world is in a rut
all this yipping
all this yapping
tantamount to heavy napping
I'd use my phone more but I'd rather not
after death my brain can rot

"You do you, completely and unabashedly."

LISA SOMERSET

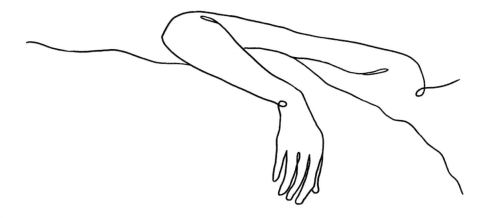

Sleep

The constant noise proves too much
In dire need of a supportive crutch

Longing for some peace and quite
Going on a life diet

Need less talk and less tv
Less mind numbing society

Putting head down to pillow
Letting all else go solo

Sleep   doze   catnap   catch some shuteye
Wave the world a temporary goodbye

Allowing thoughts to drift so deeply
Mellowed out and dreaming sweetly

Desired sleep is all encompassing
No longer feel like someone drowning

Waking up it all seems better
Walking away from bed completely unfettered

passion fruit

lustrous flavors dappled
painted with colors
so beautiful
and tasty
teasing
bright
ravishing red
flesh meets flesh
orange so ornate and opulent
there is fire in your eyes
yellow I yearn for you
peel
reveal me
gripping green
joyous
makes one want more
addictive
lick my lips
savor crave
beautiful blue
serenely sensuous
pleasingly purple
poetic
indigo on my mind

as I wrap my tongue around your words
and swallow
your brilliance
primary
secondary
tertiary
mix blend lose control
fruits
of passion

Thesaurus Poet

you abuse the English language
demean the art of words
with your addiction
to the thesaurus
replacing "abusive" with
"opprobrious"
"careful" with
"punctilious"
"gloomy" with
"saturnine"
turning a poem into a
complex formula
a language in need of
translation
tell me you're an "amateur"
not a "dilettante"
show me your "logic"
not your "ratiocination"
I want soft words with
meaning
feeling with fluid foundation
not
cement ramblings

OUTSIDE THE LINES

give me content without
"verbosity" "phraseology"
something supple yet simple
it is then "poetry"
not "patronising pretentiousness"

drying flowers

would a rose have the
same effect if I said it were a
daisy... would it smell so sweet?
would my love be accepted into
your heart if suddenly I
took it back?
and so I will. I take it back
the love I said I had for
you and now the rose smells
more like a daisy,
or does it smell at
all, before the petals
fall to the ground
and I leave you

dried.

LISA SOMERSET

far away

you are part of the stars
they have taken you
so far away
but I am still here
you too
inside me
I have lost your image
but I recall your heart
none was warmer
you made me smile on even the most gloomy of days
and even now I see you
above me
below me
beside me
within me
look...
you still make me smile
even though you are so

far away

Voltage

Our electric air makes me high
And in your energy lose control
Sanity and boredom before you came along
I welcome this eccentric chaos you bring
My life is now a poem
And you are written in my soul
I love getting crazy in your arms
And running my fingers through
That hair so untamed
It's a pure challenge
Looking into your endless eyes
Gives me a rush
Don't want to leave our world of
Fluorescent green Budweiser frogs who
Greet us in the morning as we float in the
Sky on our own private cloud
Drama/renaissance man
You're all I need/want
I kiss you with your cafe latte moustache
Until I die.

Sad But True

You're a brain breaker
Life foresaker

Narcissistic manipulator

You're a future taker
Misfortune maker

Calling all the shots perpetrator

I'm saying it
It needs to be said

You're lying in it
You've made this bed

LISA SOMERSET

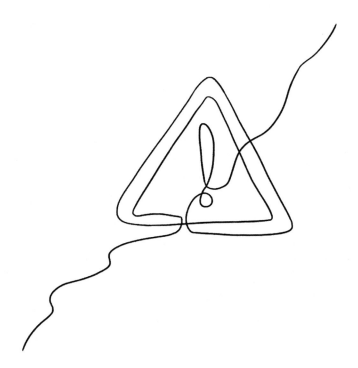

Uh Oh

We are self-destructing
Evolving   yet   devolving

On this big orb of chemicals
We are internally combusting

Our physicality phased by
mentally-draining struggles

Mindfulness fighting mindlessness
Minimalism vs maximalism

Let's pull out all the stops
This battle cannot be lost

The act of wanting more is in fact
an act of war

"Life is full of shizzle
but ya gotta find the shine."

LISA SOMERSET

Stay the course

Don't go away   or desist
Whatever the goal
       Persevere
If you want something bad enough
       You'll prevail
    Never let up
       Or allow resistance to win
Be the sole contender
    Take the prize home with you
       And keep that mentality
For always

Make It Quick

When my time comes
I want it fast

No long-term painful lingering
No skinny to skeletal

But rather blink and I'm gone
That's how I'll want it

She came   she saw
She was real   she was raw

And then she left

Aging

She's slowly changing as we all are
But what she doesn't realise is
The grace with which she enters new phases
Calmly approaching the unforeseen
Her strength as she encounters challenges
The awe that she inspires
Taking all in her stride
Going forward with a fearless head and a
Hopeful heart

Our Entirety

It's not about you
It's all around you

We're not singular
We're plural

Custodians of this planet
Looking after what for now is

Let's see beyond ourselves
At the bigger picture

Enable one another to
For a short time experience the wonder

Before the sun ever hotter
Suppers on our planetary skin

LISA SOMERSET

Find Your Flow

It's those times in between
when you're flitting to and fro

That's when you find
true meanings
It's then you find your flow

Uncertainty meets reflection
Reflection helps one grow

From unearthing deep connections
then fears we can let go

Confidence replaces dread
Procrastination fades away

That lesser self you thought you saw
is a greater self today

What It Means to Rain

(rain refurbishes the earth and nourishes the mind, giving chance to start anew)

the raindrops are my tears,
pouring and shedding my
timeless grief.
the gray clouds are my soul,
(gray because inside, you killed me).
the crashes of thunder
are my cries,
detaching my feelings from your words.
the lightening bolts are signs,
signaling it has long been time
for rain.

little tiny us

sand grain beings
living our long-short
lives
a quick exchange
humanity
circular cycles
erasing-replacing
.
.
.

being **big** by
making the most of our
little tinyness

LISA SOMERSET

Youness

In you there is a trueness
A refreshing vibrant newness

A bright openheartedness
The best sort of quirkiness

A be who you are and embrace it-ness

The woman who in the day smiles sun rays
And in the night radiates moon beams

A lioness and a goddess
Full of gracefulness and kindness

A friend filled full of friendliness

"Your brain is your life train."

Acknowledgements

I'd like to thank my family for always being there to read, listen and give honest feedback regarding my poetry; I really value their truthful opinions. The same goes for my friends who keenly welcome my poems.

In addition, I can't go without mentioning our amazing dogs: Kelly and Sonny (Labrador Retriever and Golden Retriever). Their love knows no bounds and they brighten each and every single day.

About the Author

I am originally from the USA but now live in the UK with my husband and daughter. My hobbies include writing, dog walking, watching movies and reading.

Throughout life, I've learned that there are many highs and many lows, but if we look... we can always find something to be grateful for. Often, it is the smallest of things – like a good poem!

This book is me boldly opening up the door and welcoming you to some of the thoughts from my mind. Fingers crossed certain notions resonate with you, make you feel empowered or help you to see things from a new angle.

Printed in Great Britain
by Amazon